Supermarket

Susan Canizares
Kama Einhorn

New York   Toronto   London   Auckland   Sydney
Mexico City   New Delhi   Hong Kong   Buenos Aires

PlaceBook™ Notes

Supermarkets sure are super; we can choose from over 30,000 objects to buy. That's a lot of food! Milk is the food we buy the most. It's a good thing that a cow produces enough milk in its lifetime to fill about 200,000 glasses. Cheese is another food we like to buy in the supermarket. Scientists think cheese has been around since dinosaurs roamed the earth. Cereal is also popular with supermarket shoppers. It hasn't been around as long as cheese, but when C. W. Post invented cornflakes in 1904, he was onto something. A lot of people have eaten cornflakes since 1904!

Character Design and Illustrations: James Williamson and Alex Ostroy
Book Design: James Salerno
Photo Research: Amla Sanghvi
PlaceBook Notes: Valerie Garfield

Photographs: Cover & p. 3: Kerbs/Monkmeyer; p. 4: Bill Aron/Photo Edit; p. 5: Stewart Cohen/Tony Stone; p. 6: Miro Vintoniv/Stock Boston; p. 7: Mark Segal/Tony Stone; p. 8: Mark Segal/Tony Stone; p. 9: David Young-Wolff/Photo Edit; p. 10: Mary Kate Denny/Photo Edit; p.11 Michael Newman/Photo Edit; p. 12: Chuck Keeler/Tony Stone; p. 13: Dave Rosenberg/Tony Stone; p. 14: Brady/Monkmeyer.

Copyright © 2000 by Scholastic Inc.
All rights reserved. Published by Scholastic Inc.
Printed in the U.S.A.

ISBN 0-439-62457-6

SCHOLASTIC, NINA THE NAMING NEWT, REGGIE THE RHYMING RHINO, LEO THE LETTER LOVING LOBSTER, PLACEBOOK, and associated logos and designs are trademarks and/or registered trademarks of Scholastic Inc.

3 4 5 6 7 8 9 10   23   12 11 10 09 08 07 06 05 04

It's time to go grocery shopping!

A quart of milk

and a pound of cheese are on our list.

A bag of celery

and a pound of meat are on our list.

A box of cereal

and a pound of oranges are on our list.

A dozen rolls

and a pound of fish are on our list.

It's time to check out

and take our bags.

Let's go home—and eat!

 Nina's Word Page

 cart

 fruit

 milk

 scale

 cheese

 bread

 vegetables

 cash register

Reggie's Song Page

In the Supermarket

Words and music by Fran Avni

Ni- na spies some spe- cial fruit and a loaf of bread

She loves fresh- made straw- be- rry jam be-

fore she goes to bed. Le- o the lob- ster's fee- ling fine

stand- ing in the check- out line

read- ing all the diff'rent signs in the su- per- mar- ket. In the

su- per su- per- mar- ket the su- per su- per- mar- ket in the

su- per su- per- mar- ket the su- per su- per- mar- ket.

Reggie has rhythm
He loves to rhyme
He jiggles and juggles a lemon and lime
An apple and orange, a nickel and dime